★ *GREAT SPORTS TEAMS* ★

## THE ST. LOUIS

## BASEBALL TEAM

# David Pietrusza

**Enslow Publishers, Inc.**

40 Industrial Road        PO Box 38
Box 398               Aldershot
Berkeley Heights, NJ 07922   Hants GU12 6BP
USA                           UK
http://www.enslow.com

## *Dedication*

Dr. Norton A. Karp, D.D.S.

**Library of Congress Cataloging-in-Publication Data**

Pietrusza, David, 1949–
    The St. Louis Cardinals baseball team / David Pietrusza.
        p. cm. — (Great sports teams)
    Includes bibliographical references and index.
    Summary: Surveys the history of the St. Louis Cardinals, discussing their greatest season, some of their best players, and other key personalities, including manager Whitey Herzog.
    ISBN 0-7660-1490-8
    1. St. Louis Cardinals (Baseball team)—History—Juvenile literature. [1. St. Louis Cardinals (Baseball team)—History. 2. Baseball—History.] I. Title: Saint Louis Cardinals baseball team. II. Title. III. Series.
GV875.S3 P54   2001
796.357'64'0977866—dc21

                                                    00-009113

Printed in the United States of America

10 9 8 7 6 5 4 3 2 1

**To Our Readers:** We have done our best to make sure all Internet addresses in this book were active and appropriate when we went to press. However, the author and the publisher have no control over and assume no liability for the material available on those Internet sites or on other Web sites they may link to. Any comments or suggestions can be sent by e-mail to comments@enslow.com or to the address on the back cover.

**Illustration Credits:** AP/Wide World Photos.

**Cover Illustration:** AP/Wide World Photos.

**Cover Description:** First baseman Mark McGwire.

# CONTENTS

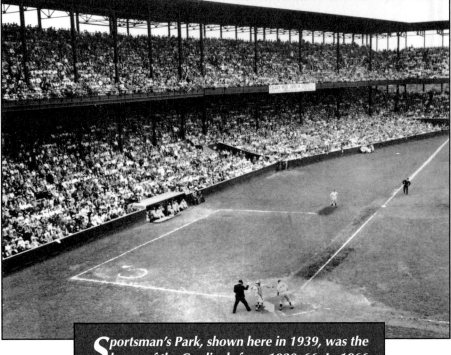

*S*portsman's Park, shown here in 1939, was the home of the Cardinals from 1920–66. In 1966 the team moved to Busch Stadium.

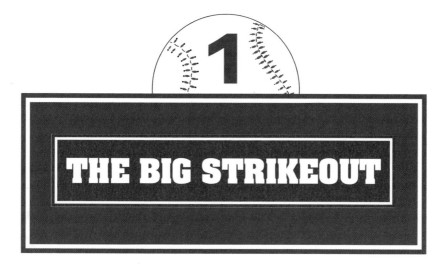

# THE BIG STRIKEOUT

On October 10, 1926, the St. Louis Cardinals were in their first-ever World Series. They had to figure out how to make the big jump from National League (NL) pennant winners to world champions.

## A Tough Opponent

It would not be easy. Player-manager Rogers Hornsby's Cardinals, also called the "Cards," were facing the New York Yankees' "Murderers Row." These big bats included outfielders Babe Ruth, Earle Combs, and Bob Meusel; first baseman Lou Gehrig; and second baseman Tony Lazzeri. The Yankees were the greatest team of the decade—some would say, of all time.

The Series was down to a deciding seventh game. In the seventh inning, the Cards were clinging to a slender 3–2 lead, but St. Louis starter Jess "Pop"

Haines was weakening. Combs led off with a single over shortstop Tommy Thevenow's head. Yankees shortstop Mark Koenig dropped a sacrifice bunt, and Combs moved to second. Haines walked Babe Ruth intentionally, putting New York runners on first and second. Bob Meusel grounded to third, forcing Ruth at second. There were now two outs, but Haines was suffering from a blister on the index finger of his pitching hand. Haines got two quick strikes on Lou Gehrig. Then he lost it completely, issuing four straight balls to walk Gehrig and load the bases.

### The Veteran

Hornsby called all his infielders in to the mound. When the conference broke up, Haines was walking off the diamond. He was out of the game. Hornsby waved to the bullpen, and brought in thirty-nine-year-old right-hander Grover Cleveland "Pete" Alexander.

Alexander was one of the game's greats. In his career he won 373 games, including 90 shutouts. Nine times he won 20 or more games. In three of those seasons, he won 30 or more contests. But his best years were behind him. Epilepsy and alcoholism had taken their toll.

There was still life in Alexander's arm. The day before, he had started Game 6 for St. Louis and defeated the Yankees, 10–2. After the game, Hornsby had told the veteran: "Alex, if you want to celebrate tonight, I wouldn't blame you. But go easy for I may need you tomorrow."[1]

*The St. Louis Cardinals Baseball Team*

**M**anager and second baseman for the St. Louis Cardinals, Rogers Hornsby, in 1926.

### Was He Ready?

Alexander did go out and celebrate, and he had spent part of the game dozing in the St. Louis bullpen. Some said he looked sluggish because he had been out late the night before. In any case, he pulled himself off the bullpen bench, and began to warm up. When Hornsby waved him in, he trudged in toward the Yankee Stadium mound.

Hornsby was waiting, and handed Alexander the ball. Then, referring to batter Tony Lazzeri and the fact that the bases were loaded, he told Alexander, "There's no place to put him."[2]

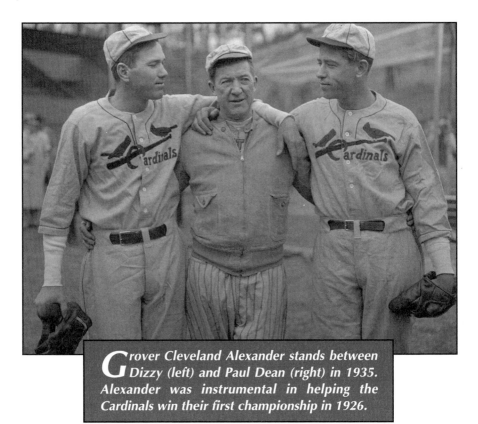

*Grover Cleveland Alexander stands between Dizzy (left) and Paul Dean (right) in 1935. Alexander was instrumental in helping the Cardinals win their first championship in 1926.*

Alexander threw a curve, and Lazzeri missed it. Lazzeri was a tough hitter. In the high minor leagues he had once hit 60 homers in a single season. Alexander's next pitch was a fastball, up and in. Lazzeri swung and drove it deep to left. He hit it so hard that there was no doubt it would clear the fence. The only question was whether it would be fair or foul. At the last minute, it hooked foul. It was just a long—and, for the Cardinals, an extremely scary—foul ball.

## Ace in the Cards

Alexander would not throw another curve if he could help it. Lazzeri swung at the next pitch, and missed. The inning was over! The Cards were out of the jam.

It would take another two innings of hitless work for Alexander to nail down the save, but the Lazzeri strikeout broke the back of the Yankees' comeback attempt. The St. Louis Cardinals—once yearly also-rans in the National League—were the world champions.

This was only the first championship for what has become one of major-league baseball's most successful franchises.

*T*he Cardinals' Gas House Gang of 1934
included (from left to right) pitchers Dizzy
and Paul Dean, manager Frankie Frisch, and
catcher Bill DeLancey.

**MEET ME IN ST. LOUIS**

**T**he St. Louis Cardinals formed back in 1882. They played in the old American Association (AA), which was then a major-league rival of the National League. The team was known as the Browns, and was owned by a colorful German-born local saloon keeper, Chris Von der Ahe.

### A Good Start

Von der Ahe did some questionable things, but he was smart enough to hire savvy first baseman Charles Comiskey as his manager. Under Comiskey, the Browns won AA pennants in 1885, 1886, 1887, and 1888.

When the American Association went out of business after the 1891 season, the team became a member of the National League. For the next three decades, the franchise fared poorly. Then new owner "Singing Sam" Breadon arrived on the scene. He hired General

Manager Branch Rickey and heavy-hitting player-manager Rogers Hornsby. Soon the Cardinals became winners.

Rickey and Breadon instituted the farm system, and talent poured into St. Louis's Sportsman's Park from the team's minor-league teams. Hornsby hit .400 for St. Louis—not just once, but three times. The Cardinals won the World Series in 1926, but Breadon had already grown tired of Hornsby. He not only fired him as manager; he traded him to the New York Giants for another second baseman, speedy Frankie Frisch.

### Gas House Gang

St. Louis fans were incensed, but Frisch turned out to be a great replacement for Hornsby. "In all the years I have had with the Cardinals," Breadon later said, "no player ever played such ball for me as did Frank Frisch in 1927."[1]

Frisch won over the fans, and the Cardinals won NL pennants in 1928, 1930, and 1931. By 1933, Breadon had named Frisch as Cards manager. The team was now known as the Gas House Gang because of the rough-and-tumble way it played ball. Left fielder Joe "Ducky" Medwick, pitchers Wild Bill Hallahan and Dizzy and Daffy Dean, shortstop Leo "the Lip" Durocher, and third baseman Pepper Martin did all they could to win. In 1934, they defeated the Detroit Tigers in one of the rowdiest World Series ever.

L eo "the Lip" Durocher played shortstop for the Cardinals on the 1934 World Series Championship team.

### Stan the Man

The Cardinals did not win another World Series until the 1940s. By this time, outfielders Stan Musial, Terry Moore, and Enos Slaughter had arrived, as well as slick fielding shortstop Marty Marion. Said legendary Philadelphia A's manager Connie Mack, "There is no doubt in my mind that Marion is the greatest living shortstop, perhaps the greatest of all time."[2]

In the early 1940s, St. Louis dominated the National League. They won a team-record 106 games in 1941.

That season, they tied the Brooklyn Dodgers for first and then lost a postseason playoff. In both 1943 and 1944, the Cardinals won 105 games. They captured pennants in 1942, 1943, 1944, and 1946. In 1944, they defeated their St. Louis rivals, the American League's Browns, in the only all–St. Louis World Series ever. In 1946, they won another World Championship, defeating the Boston Red Sox in one of baseball's most exciting World Series. "What made the Cardinals special," said Enos Slaughter, "was that we were a team of players who always felt we could win. No matter how far we were down, or regardless of who had been sold or injured, we always thought that we could beat anybody."[3]

## New Home

The 1950s Cardinals teams—despite having such fine players as Musial and third baseman Ken Boyer—always finished out of the running. Yet things were changing in Cardinals history. After the 1952 season, the Browns left town and became the Baltimore Orioles. The Redbirds now had St. Louis all to themselves. In 1966, the team moved from the old Sportsman's Park (where they had played since 1920) to the new Busch Stadium in downtown St. Louis.

## 1960s Success

Not until 1964 would the Cards, helped by newcomers Bob Gibson and Lou Brock, win another World Series. They defeated Yogi Berra and the rest of the New York Yankees in seven games. The Cards took another

*O*utfielder Enos Slaughter helped the St. Louis Cardinals dominate the National League in the early 1940s.

world championship in 1967, defeating the Red Sox in another seven-game series. Gibson won three games in that year's World Series. The Cards won another pennant the following year, but lost the 1968 Series to the Detroit Tigers.

Of the 1967 Cards, Bob Gibson wrote, "I know that every player who came over from another team. . .all of them said the same thing. They [had] never been with a team that had as much spirit as our team."[4]

*S*tan "the Man" Musial had 3,630 hits and 475 home runs in his career. He won the MVP Award three times and was named as an all-star twenty-four times.

# CARDINALS IMMORTALS

The Cardinals have boasted many fine players in their long history. The performers described in this chapter have either already been elected to the Baseball Hall of Fame or—in the case of fine-fielding shortstop Ozzie Smith—certainly will be.

## *Rogers Hornsby*

When it came to hitting for average, Rogers Hornsby was the greatest right-handed hitter in major-league history. He hit .358 over the course of his career. He batted over .400 three times—.401 (in 1922 when he won the NL Triple Crown), .424 (in 1924), and .403 (in 1925). The Texas-born second baseman won six batting crowns, including five in a row. Nine times he led the league in slugging. Eight times he paced it in on-base percentage. But his stubborn and blunt attitude caused him to be traded from club to club.

"I always said what was on my mind," he once remarked. "I told the truth as I saw it. I was raised that way. I couldn't do any different than that."[1] Despite his controversial nature, he was elected to the Hall of Fame in 1942.

### Dizzy Dean

Dizzy Dean, who won 30 games in 1934, was one of the most colorful people ever to play the game. Dean might have recorded many more fine years had he not injured his toe in the 1937 All-Star game. That mishap led to a serious arm injury that ended his effectiveness. Once, in the second game of a doubleheader against the Dodgers, Dizzy's brother Paul "Daffy" Dean pitched a no-hitter. Dizzy had three-hit Brooklyn in the first game. "Shucks, Paul, why didn't you tell me you was gonna do that?" Dean asked his brother. "I'd have pitched one too."[2] He was elected to the Hall of Fame in 1953.

### Stan Musial

They first called Stan Musial "the Man" because he was the man who demolished Brooklyn Dodger pitching. Before he was through, he had demolished all National League pitching, posting a lifetime .331 average. He appeared in 24 All-Star games, won three MVP awards, hit 475 homers, and accumulated 3,630 hits. "How good was Stan Musial?" Dodgers broadcaster Vin Scully asked, long after Musial had retired. "He was good enough to take your breath away."[3] Musial was elected to the Hall of Fame in 1969.

### Enos Slaughter

Cardinals outfielder Enos "Country" Slaughter was noted for his tough, hard-nosed style of play. His hustling baserunning in the 1946 World Series helped give St. Louis the world championship over the Boston Red Sox. Slaughter led the National League with 130 RBIs in 1946 and posted a lifetime .300 average. The North Carolina native was elected to the Hall of Fame in 1985.

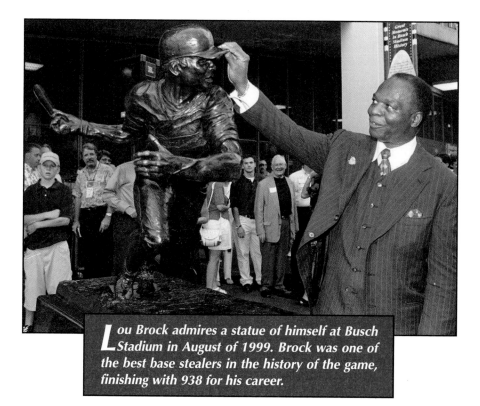

Lou Brock admires a statue of himself at Busch Stadium in August of 1999. Brock was one of the best base stealers in the history of the game, finishing with 938 for his career.

### Lou Brock

Lou Brock ranks as one of the greatest base stealers of all time. In his early years with the Chicago Cubs, Brock barely looked like a big-leaguer. Soon after being traded to the Cardinals, he proved his critics wrong. He stole 118 bases, then a major-league record, during the 1974 season, and swiped a total of 938 bags in his career. Brock, who also recorded his 3,000th hit in 1974, won election to the Hall of Fame in 1985.

### Bob Gibson

Bob Gibson posted solid statistics throughout his long career, but there is no doubt which season was his best. In 1968, he won the MVP award, pitched 28 complete games and 13 shutouts—and set a National League record with a 1.12 ERA. For his career, he won nine Gold Glove Awards and two Cy Young Awards. He was 7–2 in World Series competition and struck out 17 batters in one game during the 1968 World Series. "Gibson had that deadly combination of speed and pinpoint control," Nolan Ryan once wrote.[4] Gibson was inducted into the Hall of Fame in 1981.

### Ozzie Smith

Ozzie Smith won 13 straight Gold Gloves, each year from 1980 to 1992. That is the longest string by any major-league shortstop. "I'd like to be remembered as a player who helped show people the importance of defense," he wrote in his autobiography, "and help defensive players earn some of the recognition and money usually reserved for offensive players."[5] The

*The St. Louis Cardinals Baseball Team*

*B*ob Gibson pitched 28 complete games and 13 shutouts in his spectacular 1968 season.

"Wizard of Oz" certainly accomplished that, being recognized by many as the greatest defensive player in baseball history. Along the way, he developed into a crafty base stealer and a more than adequate hitter. Smith becomes eligible for the Hall of Fame in 2002.

*C*ardinals General Manager Branch Rickey stands alongside pitcher Paul Dean in this photo from 1938.

# CARDINALS LEADERSHIP

ome outstanding leaders have guided the Cardinals franchise. Many have even been enshrined in the Hall of Fame.

## *Branch Rickey*

In 1999, ESPN took a poll to find out who the public thought was the most influential sports figure of the century. The winner: Branch Rickey, the man who integrated major-league baseball when he brought Jackie Robinson to the Brooklyn Dodgers in 1947.

Rickey had a long and very successful career with the Cardinals before he became Brooklyn's general manager. As the St. Louis general manager, he invented the farm system and made the Redbirds a National League powerhouse. Under Rickey they won pennants in five of nine seasons, from 1926 through 1934. Other Rickey innovations included Ladies Day, the batting cage, and the Knothole Gang. Toward the end of his career, he helped force major-league baseball's first expansion. Branch Rickey was elected to the Hall of Fame in 1967.

### Bill McKechnie

Bill McKechnie is the only National League manager to win pennants with three different teams—the Pirates, Reds, and Cardinals. With St. Louis he won in 1928 but lost in four games to the Yankees in the World Series. Owner Sam Breadon then demoted McKechnie to the minors. He soon brought him back, however. McKechnie was elected to the Hall of Fame in 1962.

### Frankie Frisch

Frankie Frisch was not only a successful Cards manager; he was also one of baseball's greatest second basemen, hitting .300 for eleven straight years. Yet his arrival in St. Louis was controversial, since he was traded for the popular Rogers Hornsby. In 1934, Frisch managed the St. Louis Gas House Gang to the National League pennant and a World Series win over Detroit. He was elected to the Hall of Fame in 1947.

### Billy Southworth

Billy Southworth is almost forgotten today, but in his time he was one of baseball's finest managers. His lifetime major-league record is 1,064 wins against only 729 losses. With St. Louis he won three straight pennants, from 1942 through 1944, and two world championships. He led the Boston Braves to an NL pennant in 1948.

*The St. Louis Cardinals Baseball Team*

### Eddie Dyer

In 1946, Eddie Dyer's first year as a major-league manager, he won a world championship with the Cards. It certainly was not an easy task. At season's end, Brooklyn and St. Louis were tied for first, and the Cards had to win the first postseason playoff in major-league history to earn the pennant. In the World Series, it went down to the wire against the Red Sox, helped by Enos Slaughter's great baserunning in the seventh game.

### Johnnie Keane

The 1964 version of the Cardinals did not look likely to win, so team owner Gussie Busch planned to fire manager Johnny Keane at season's end. But Keane's Cards surprised everyone. They not only won the pennant; they beat the Yankees in the World Series. Keane, however, knew about Busch's plans and was not happy. He quit as St. Louis manager. Since the Yankees had just fired their manager, Yogi Berra, Keane ended up piloting New York, replacing Berra.

### Red Schoendienst

As Cards manager, Red Schoendienst won pennants in 1967 and 1968 and a World Championship in 1967. Like Frankie Frisch, he was also a superb second baseman. The popular Schoendienst, also a longtime Cardinals coach, was elected to the Hall of Fame in 1989.

### Whitey Herzog

They called Whitey Herzog's style of managing Whiteyball, and it worked like a charm in both Kansas City and St. Louis. Whiteyball emphasized speed and defense. Players such as Keith Hernandez, shortstop Ozzie Smith, and outfielders Vince Coleman and Willie McGee fit his system well. Whitey's Cards won

*Whitey Herzog (left) led the Cardinals to the World Series in 1982, 1985, and 1987. The team won it all in 1982.*

*The St. Louis Cardinals Baseball Team*

*T*ony LaRussa led the Cardinals to NL Central titles in 1996 and 2000.

a world championship in 1982 and two more pennants in 1985 and 1987.

### Tony LaRussa

Like Branch Rickey (and another Cards manager, Miller Huggins) Tony LaRussa is one of the few attorneys to manage in the major leagues. LaRussa enjoyed his greatest success as manager of the Oakland A's, but he also captured NL Central titles in 1996 and 2000. Perhaps LaRussa's finest accomplishment as a Cardinal, however, is helping to entice homerun king Mark McGwire to join the team.

*W*hitey Herzog's Cardinals teams of the 1980s focused on speed and pitching to take advantage of the cavernous Busch Stadium.

## WHITEYBALL

**A**fter the Cards won the pennant in 1968, the team went into a long period of decline. It was not until former Kansas City Royals manager Dorrel Norman "Whitey" Herzog became the Cardinals skipper in 1980 that the team returned to its winning ways.

### Speed and Defense

Herzog believed in combining speed and defense to win ball games. In the 1980s, players such as shortstop Ozzie Smith; outfielders Lonnie Smith, Willie McGee, and Vince Coleman; first baseman Keith Hernandez; catcher Darrell Porter; and second baseman Tommy Herr supplied the Cardinals with that formula. Outfielder George Hendrick and, later, first baseman Jack Clark added a dash of power. Bob Forsch, Joaquin Andujar, John Tudor, and reliever Bruce Sutter provided the pitching. To assemble that winning combination, Herzog had to restructure almost the entire team. "We cleaned house," wrote Herzog, "got the speed, relief pitching, and catching we needed. More importantly, we had twenty-five good guys on the club,. . . no more prima donnas."[1]

Under Herzog the 1981 Cards had the best won-lost record in the NL East. Because of that season's players' strike, the season was split into two halves. The Cards finished second in both halves, and did not see postseason action.

### Suds Series

In 1982, the Cards edged out the Philadelphia Phillies in the NL East, hitting just 68 homers but swiping a league-leading 200 stolen bases. Then St. Louis swept the Atlanta Braves in the National League Championship Series (NLCS). In the World Series, they faced the American League's hard-hitting Milwaukee Brewers. It became known as the Suds Series because both teams were owned by beer manufacturers.

The Series went into the seventh game. The Brewers took a 3–1 lead into the sixth inning. Then, Keith Hernandez drove in two runs to tie the score, and George Hendrick singled in a go-ahead run. The final score was Cards 6, Brewers 3. St. Louis was world champion.

### Back on Top

The Cards fell back during the next few seasons. Part of the problem was Hernandez, who had off-the-field

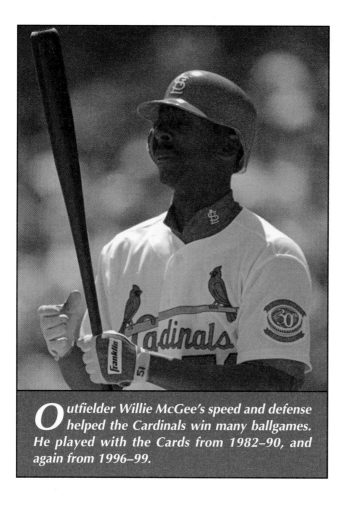

*O* utfielder Willie McGee's speed and defense
helped the Cardinals win many ballgames.
*He played with the Cards from 1982–90, and
again from 1996–99.*

problems. Herzog, who would not tolerate such
behavior, traded him to the Mets. To replace
Hernandez, Herzog obtained first baseman Jack Clark
from the San Francisco Giants. According to Herzog,
Clark was "the best clutch hitter in baseball."[2] By 1985,
Vince Coleman had reached the majors, and he stole
110 bases in his rookie season. McGee led the league
with a .353 average, 216 hits, and 18 triples and won
the National League MVP award. John Tudor led the
league with 10 shutouts. St. Louis was ready to return
to the postseason.

*T*he "Wizard of Oz," Ozzie Smith, is considered by many to be the greatest defensive shortstop of all time.

The Cards sneaked past the Mets in the NL East. Then they defeated the Los Angeles Dodgers in the NLCS, before facing the Kansas City Royals in the World Series. This series was nicknamed the I-90 Series, after the interstate highway that connected St. Louis with Kansas City, Missouri. The Cards jumped off to a three- games-to-one lead but could not put the Royals away. The Series reached a seventh game, which was a complete disaster for St. Louis. The Royals scored eleven runs off seven Cardinals pitchers.

*The St. Louis Cardinals Baseball Team*

One pitcher, Joaquin Andujar, was even ejected from the game. The Royals won by a final score of 11–0.

## End of an Era

Jack Clark was injured for much of 1986, but he and Vince Coleman had excellent seasons in 1987. Their efforts powered the team to another division title, again after a tight duel with the Mets. In the NLCS, St. Louis beat the Giants in seven games. The Cards then faced the Minnesota Twins in the World Series. It was an unusual series, because the home team won in every contest. That translated into a Twins victory in seven games.

That was the Cards' last pennant of the twentieth century. In 1989, longtime team owner August A. Busch III died. The next year, Whitey Herzog resigned as manager. A new Cardinals era would soon begin. It would be the Era of McGwire.

*McGwire is shown here connecting for his 70th home run in the Cardinals last game of the 1998 season. McGwire's 70 home runs set a new record for home runs in a season.*

# A MAN NAMED MCGWIRE

**T**he 1990s were not the greatest of decades for the Cardinals franchise, but there were some highlights. In 1996, manager Tony LaRussa led the team to first place in the National League's Central Division. The Cards finished 88–74, winning the division by six games. The Cards swept the San Diego Padres in three games in the National League Division Series, but the team lost the NLCS to the Atlanta Braves in seven games. After five games, St. Louis led the Braves, 3–2—but then Atlanta got serious. They won game five, 14–0, and game seven, 15–0.

## *Big Red*

The Cardinals would not reach the postseason again in the 1990s. Still, the decade did not lack excitement.

In July 1997, the Cards obtained slugging first baseman Mark McGwire from the American League's Oakland A's. The price was low: pitchers T. J. Mathews,

Eric Ludwick, and Blake Stein. Cards manager Tony LaRussa, who had managed McGwire in Oakland, knew the muscular slugger would fit in with his new team. "The one thing he does that's. . . most impressive. . . is talk to the other guys about the right way to be a professional winning player," said LaRussa about McGwire. "He'll go to them and talk to them about things like taking a pitch when the team is behind, playing through minor injuries, hitting to the opposite field. And he likes to talk, to teach, and really get involved."[1]

## *The Longball*

When the trade took place on July 31, 1997, McGwire had already hit 34 homers that season. With the Cards he added another 24—for a impressive total of 58.

In the off-season everyone asked the same question about this powerful redheaded slugger: Could he break Roger Maris's single-season record of 61 homers in 1998?

McGwire would have some tough competition in the homer-hitting business. Outfielders Sammy Sosa of the Chicago Cubs and Ken Griffey, Jr., of the Seattle Mariners were also considered capable of breaking the record. McGwire started the season with a grand slam on Opening Day 1998 and never looked back. He had 11 dingers at the end of April, 27 at the end of May, 37 at the end of June, and 45 at the end of July.

## Home Run King

McGwire tied Maris's record on September 7—and broke the record the next night, off Chicago Cubs pitcher Steve Trachsel. The forty thousand fans at Busch Stadium cheered for eleven minutes. "I hope someday my son grows up to be a baseball player and breaks the record," said McGwire.[2]

*Mark McGwire is hugged by Chicago Cubs outfielder Sammy Sosa after hitting his record-breaking 62nd home run on September 8, 1998.*

There was still a fair amount of the season to go, however. McGwire seemed to tire, and suddenly Sosa began to pick up steam. It looked as if Sosa might pass McGwire for the ultimate record. "Wouldn't it be great if we just ended up tied?" commented McGwire, who enjoyed a warm friendship with Sosa.[3] On September 25, Sosa hit number 66, to pass McGwire. Then, just forty-five minutes later, McGwire homered to tie Sosa. He went deep twice more the following day. The day after that (the final day of the season), he hit another

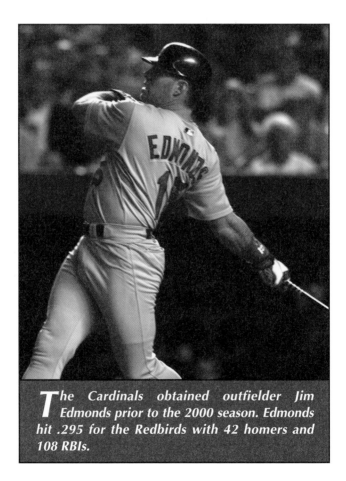

*The Cardinals obtained outfielder Jim Edmonds prior to the 2000 season. Edmonds hit .295 for the Redbirds with 42 homers and 108 RBIs.*

*The St. Louis Cardinals Baseball Team*

pair of four-baggers—giving him the amazing total of 70 homers for a single season.

No one had ever believed that anyone—even the Babe or Roger Maris—could hit 70 homers in a season. Mark McGwire had accomplished the impossible.

## Among the Greats

In 1999, McGwire proved—as if he had to—that his slugging was no fluke. He slammed 65 homers and drove in a career-high 147 RBIs. He moved past Hall of Famers Ted Williams and Willie McCovey for tenth place on the all-time home run list. The Cardinals finished a disappointing fourth in the NL Central Division.

In 2000 the Cards returned to the top of the NL Central. Injuries hobbled McGwire and he finished the year with just 32 homers and 73 RBIs. Picking up the slack were pitcher Darryl Kile (20-9, 3.91 ERA) and recently acquired outfielder Jim Edmonds (42 HR, 108 RBIs, .295).

St. Louis remains a great baseball town, and there is no doubt that the city's team will have many more first-place finishes in its future. It is just the Cardinal way.

# STATISTICS

## Team Record

### The Cardinals History

| YEARS | W | L | PCT. | PENNANTS | WORLD SERIES |
|---|---|---|---|---|---|
| 1890s | 400 | 707 | .361 | None | None |
| 1900–09 | 580 | 888 | .395 | None | None |
| 1910–19 | 652 | 830 | .440 | None | None |
| 1920–29 | 822 | 712 | .536 | 1926, 1928 | 1926 |
| 1930–39 | 869 | 665 | .566 | 1930–31, 1934 | 1931, 1934 |
| 1940–49 | 960 | 580 | .623 | 1942–44, 1946 | 1942, 1944, 1946 |
| 1950–59 | 776 | 763 | .504 | None | None |
| 1960–69 | 884 | 718 | .552 | 1964, 1967–68 | 1964, 1967 |
| 1970–79 | 800 | 813 | .496 | None | None |
| 1980–89 | 825 | 734 | .529 | 1982, 1985, 1987 | 1982 |
| 1990–99 | 757 | 794 | .488 | None | None |
| 2000– | 95 | 67 | .586 | None | None |

### The Cardinals Today

| YEAR | W | L | PCT. | MANAGER | |
|---|---|---|---|---|---|
| 1990 | 70 | 92 | .432 | Whitey Herzog, Red Schoendienst, Joe Torre | 6 |
| 1991 | 84 | 78 | .519 | Joe Torre | 2 |
| 1992 | 83 | 79 | .512 | Joe Torre | 3 |
| 1993 | 87 | 75 | .537 | Joe Torre | 3 |
| 1994 | 53 | 61 | .465 | Joe Torre | 3 |
| 1995 | 62 | 81 | .434 | Joe Torre, Mike Jorgensen | 4 |
| 1996 | 88 | 74 | .543 | Tony LaRussa | 1 |
| 1997 | 73 | 89 | .451 | Tony LaRussa | 4 |
| 1998 | 83 | 79 | .512 | Tony LaRussa | 3 |
| 1999 | 75 | 86 | .466 | Tony LaRussa | 4 |
| 2000 | 95 | 67 | .586 | Tony LaRussa | 1 |

*The St. Louis Cardinals Baseball Team*

## Total History

| W | L | PCT | PENNANTS | WORLD SERIES |
|---|---|-----|----------|--------------|
| 8,420 | 8,271 | .504 | 15 | 9 |

W=Wins
L=Losses
PCT=Winning Percentage

PENNANTS=Won NL title
WORLD SERIES=Won World Series

## Championship Managers

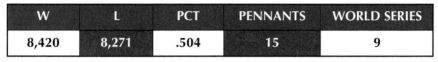

| MANAGER | YEARS MANAGED | RECORD* | PENNANTS | WORLD SERIES |
|---------|---------------|---------|----------|--------------|
| Rogers Hornsby | 1925–26 | 153–116 | 1 | 1 |
| Bill McKechnie | 1928–29 | 129–88 | 1 | 0 |
| Billy Southworth | 1929, 1940–45 | 620–346 | 3 | 2 |
| Gabby Street | 1929, 1930–33 | 312–242 | 2 | 1 |
| Frankie Frisch | 1933–38 | 458–354 | 1 | 1 |
| Eddie Dyer | 1946–50 | 446–325 | 1 | 1 |
| Johnny Keane | 1962–64 | 317–249 | 1 | 1 |
| Red Schoendienst | 1965–76, 1980, 1990 | 1,041–955 | 2 | 1 |
| Whitey Herzog | 1981–90 | 822–728 | 3 | 1 |

*=Record with Cardinals

## Great Hitters

| PLAYER | SEA | YRS | G | AB | R | H | HR | RBI | SB | AVG |
|---|---|---|---|---|---|---|---|---|---|---|
| Jim Bottomley* | 1922–32 | 16 | 1,991 | 7,471 | 1,177 | 2,313 | 219 | 1,422 | 58 | .31( |
| Lou Brock* | 1964–79 | 19 | 2,616 | 10,332 | 1,610 | 3,023 | 149 | 900 | 938 | .29' |
| Frankie Frisch* | 1927–37 | 19 | 2,311 | 9,112 | 1,532 | 2,880 | 105 | 1,244 | 419 | .31( |
| Rogers Hornsby* | 1915–26, 1933 | 23 | 2,259 | 8,173 | 1,579 | 2,930 | 301 | 1,584 | 135 | .35{ |
| Mark McGwire | 1997– | 15 | 1,777 | 5,888 | 1,119 | 1,570 | 554 | 1,350 | 12 | .26' |
| Joe Medwick* | 1932–40, 1947–48 | 17 | 1,964 | 7,635 | 1,198 | 2,471 | 205 | 1,383 | 42 | .32 |
| Johnny Mize* | 1936–41 | 15 | 1,884 | 6,443 | 1,118 | 2,011 | 359 | 1,337 | 28 | .31 |
| Stan Musial* | 1941–44, 1946–63 | 22 | 3,026 | 10,972 | 1,949 | 3,630 | 475 | 1,951 | 78 | .33 |
| Enos Slaughter* | 1938–42, 1946–53 | 19 | 2,380 | 7,946 | 1,247 | 2,383 | 169 | 1,304 | 71 | .30( |
| Ozzie Smith | 1982–96 | 19 | 2,573 | 9,396 | 1,257 | 2,460 | 28 | 793 | 580 | .26 |

**SEA**=Season with Cardinals
**YRS**=Years in Majors
**G**=Games
**AB**=At-bats

**R**=Runs
**H**=Hits
**HR**=Home Runs
**RBI**=Runs Batted In

**SB**=Stolen Bases
**AVG**=Batting Average
*=Member of National Baseball Hall of Fame

## Great Pitchers — CAREER STATISTICS

| PLAYER | SEA | YRS | W | L | PCT | ERA | G | SV | IP | K | SH |
|---|---|---|---|---|---|---|---|---|---|---|---|
| GC Alexander* | 4 | 20 | 373 | 208 | .642 | 2.56 | 696 | 32 | 5,190 | 2,198 | 90 |
| Steve Carlton* | 7 | 24 | 329 | 244 | .574 | 3.22 | 741 | 2 | 5,217.1 | 4,136 | 55 |
| Dizzy Dean* | 7 | 12 | 150 | 83 | .644 | 3.02 | 317 | 30 | 1,967.1 | 1,163 | 26 |
| Bob Gibson* | 17 | 17 | 251 | 174 | .591 | 2.91 | 528 | 6 | 3,884.1 | 3,117 | 56 |
| Lee Smith | 4 | 18 | 71 | 92 | .436 | 3.03 | 1,022 | 478 | 1,290 | 1,251 | 0 |

**SEA**=Season with Cardinals
**YRS**=Years in Majors
**W**=Wins
**L**=Losses

**PCT**=Winning Percentage
**ERA**=Earned Run Average
**G**=Games
**SV**=Saves

**IP**=Innings Pitched
**K**=Strikeouts
**SH**=Shutouts
*=Member of National Baseball Hall of Fame

*The St. Louis Cardinals Baseball Team*

# CHAPTER NOTES

### Chapter 1. The Big Strikeout

1. Eliot Cohen, ed., *My Greatest Day in Baseball* (New York: Simon & Schuster, 1991), p. 6.

2. Tom Meany, *Baseball's Greatest Pitchers* (New York: A. S. Barne, 1951), p. 9.

### Chapter 2. Meet Me in St. Louis

1. Frederick C. Lieb, *The St. Louis Cardinals* (New York: G. P. Putnam's Sons, (1945), p. 130.

2. Donald Honig, *The Greatest Shortstops of All Time* (Dubuque, Iowa: Brown & Benchmark, 1992), p. 65.

3. Enos Slaughter with Kevin Reid, *Country Hardball* (Greensboro, N.C.: Tudor Publishing, 1991), pp. 61–62.

4. Bob Gibson with Phil Pepe, *From Ghetto to Glory* (New York: Popular Library, 1968), p. 123.

### Chapter 3. Cardinal Immortals

1. Tom Murray, ed., *Sport Magazine's All-Time All Stars* (New York: New American Library, 1977), p. 246.

2. Rob Rains, *The St. Louis Cardinals* (New York: St. Martin's, 1992), p. 72.

3. Paul Dickson, *Baseball's Greatest Quotations* (New York: HarperCollins, 1991), p. 387.

4. Nolan Ryan and Mickey Herskowitz, *Kings of the Hill* (New York: HarperPaperbacks, 1992), p. 114.

5. Ozzie Smith with Rob Rains, *Wizard* (Chicago: Contemporary Books, 1988), p. 187.

### Chapter 5. Whiteyball

1. White Herzog and Kevin Horrigan, *White Rat: A Life in Baseball* (New York: Harper & Row, 1987), p. 139.

2. Donald Honig, *The St. Louis Cardinals: An Illustrated History* (New York: Prentice Hall, 1991), p. 219.

### Chapter 6. A Man Named McGwire

1. Rob Rains, *Mark McGwire: Home Run Hero* (New York: St. Martin's, 1998), p. 206.

2. Lee R. Schreiber, *Race for the Record: The Great Home Run Chase of 1998* (New York: HarperPerennial, 1998), p. 85.

3. Ibid., p. 14.

# GLOSSARY

**American Association**—A defunct major league that operated from 1882 through 1891.

**American League**—One of the two current major leagues of baseball, founded in 1901 by Ban Johnson.

**batting average**—At-bats divided by hits.

**Cy Young Award**— Award given each year to the best pitcher in each major league.

**designated hitter**—A player who bats, but who does not take the field during the game. In the major leagues, the designated hitter (DH) is used only in American League ballparks.

**epilepsy**—A type of nervous disorder with symptoms of seizures, convulsions and a loss of consciousness.

**ERA (Earned Run Average)**—The number of earned runs divided by the number of innings pitched times nine; the ERA is perhaps the best measure of pitching effectiveness.

**free agent**—A major-leaguer whose contractual obligations to his old team have expired and who is free to sign with another team.

**General Manager**—The official in charge of a ball club's business and personnel matters.

**Gold Glove Award**—Award given annually to the best fielder at each position in both the National and American Leagues.

**infielder**—One who plays an infield position (first, second, or third base or shortstop).

**Knothole Gang**—A promotion in which children are allowed into a game for free.

**League Championship Series**—The best-of-seven series that determines the American and National League champions.

**National League**—The oldest surviving major league, founded in 1876 by William Hulbert. Sometimes called the senior circuit.

**pennant**—A league championship, alternately called the flag.

**RBI**—Run batted in.

**stolen base**—A play in which the base runner advances to another base while the pitcher takes his motion.

**wildcard**—The non-division-winning club with the best won-lost percentage in regular-season play; the wildcard team in each league earns a berth in postseason play.

# FURTHER READING

Deane, Bill. *Bob Gibson (Baseball Legends)*. New York: Chelsea House, 1994.

Eisenbath, Mike. *The Cardinals Encyclopedia*. Philadelphia: Temple University Press, 1999.

Gibson, Bob, with Phil Pepe. *From Ghetto to Glory*. New York: Popular Library, 1968.

Goodman, Michael E. *The History of the St. Louis Cardinals*. Mankato, Minn.: The Creative Company, 1998.

Grabowski, John. *Stan Musial (Baseball Legends)*. New York: Chelsea House, 1993.

Kavanagh, Jack. *Ol' Pete: The Grover Cleveland Alexander Story*. South Bend, Ind.: Diamond Communications, 1996.

Musial, Stan, as told to Bob Broeg. *Stan Musial: "The Man's" Own Story*. New York: Doubleday, 1964.

Pietrusza, David. *Top 10 Baseball Managers*. Springfield, N.J.: Enslow Publishers, Inc., 1998.

Rains, Rob. *Mark McGwire: Home Run Hero*. New York: St Martin's, 1998.

Schreiber, Lee R. *Race for the Record: The Great Home Run Chase of 1998*. New York: HarperPerennial, 1998.

Sehnert, Chris W. *St. Louis Cardinals*. Minneapolis: ABDO Publishing Company, 1997.

Smith, Ozzie. *Wizard*. Chicago: Contemporary Books, 1988.

Thorn, John, et al., eds. *Total Baseball*. Seventh edition. Kingston, N.Y.: Total Sports Publishing, 2001.

Thornley, Stew. *Mark McGwire: Star Home Run Hitter*. Berkeley Heights, N.J.: Enslow Publishers, Inc., 1999.

# INDEX

# WHERE TO WRITE AND INTERNET SITES

**Official site of the St. Louis Cardinals**
http://cardinals.mlb.com/
NASApp/mlb/stl/homepages/
stl_homepage.jsp

**Major League Baseball's Cardinals Team Page**
http://baseball.espn.go.com/
mlb/clubhouse?team=stl

**ESPN's Mark McGwire Profile**
http://espn.go.com/mlb/profiles/profile/3866.html

**Stan Musial Official Baseball Site**
http://www.stan-the-man.com/

St. Louis Cardinals
250 Stadium Plaza
St. Louis, MO 63102